Arthur Hugh Clough

by ISOBEL ARMSTRONG

Published for The British Council
and The National Book League
by Longmans, Green & Co.

Two shillings and sixpence net

Mrs. Isobel Armstrong has as her subject one of the less well-known but very significant Victorian poets, Arthur Hugh Clough (1819-1861). Clough, a product of Arnold of Rugby and of Balliol College, Oxford, became a Fellow of Oriel, then, after throwing up his Fellowship, was offered the Principalship of University Hall, London. He was later an examiner in the Education Office, and died, very young, at Florence. His fine lyrics include the very well-known 'Say not the struggle nought availeth' and Matthew Arnold's 'Thyrsis' was written to commemorate his death.

Mrs. Armstrong's is a very full survey of every aspect of Clough's work, and her bibliography is even more detailed than is usual in this series. She is a graduate of the University of Leicester and is working at present on nineteenth century poetry.

Bibliographical Series
of Supplements to 'British Book News'
on Writers and their Work

★

GENERAL EDITOR
Bonamy Dobrée

Arthur Hugh Clough

From a chalk drawing of about 1860 by S. Rowse in the
National Portrait Gallery

ARTHUR HUGH CLOUGH

by

ISOBEL ARMSTRONG

Published for the British Council and
The National Book League by
LONGMANS GREEN & CO.

LONGMANS, GREEN & CO. LTD.,
48 Grosvenor Street, London, W.1.
Railway Crescent, Croydon, Victoria, Australia
Auckland, Kingston (Jamaica), Lahore, Nairobi

LONGMANS SOUTHERN AFRICA (PTY) LTD.
Thibault House, Thibault Square, Cape Town,
Johannesburg, Salisbury

LONGMANS OF NIGERIA LTD.
W.R. Industrial Estate, Ikeja

LONGMANS OF GHANA LTD.
Industrial Estate, Ring Road South, Accra

LONGMANS GREEN (FAR EAST) LTD.
443 Lockhart Road, Hong Kong

LONGMANS OF MALAYA LTD.
44 Jalan Ampang, Kuala Lumpur

ORIENT LONGMANS LTD.
Calcutta, Bombay, Madras
Delhi, Hyderabad, Dacca

LONGMANS CANADA LTD.
137 Bond Street, Toronto 2

First published in 1962
© Isobel Armstrong, 1962

Printed in Great Britain by
*F. Mildner & Sons, London, E.C.*1

Contents

¶ Arthur Hugh Clough was born on 1 Jan. 1819 and died on 13 Nov., 1861. He is buried in the Protestant cemetary at Florence.

A. H. CLOUGH

I. INTRODUCTION

(i) Life

CLOUGH has until recently been regarded as a marginal and eccentric poet. Yet he is in no sense a peripheral writer. His work is unique in Victorian poetry, and he developed a remarkably individual idiom.

Even a new reader of Clough soon learns to recognise his characteristic tones and manners of approach:

> So that the whole great wicked artificial civilised fabric—
> All its unfinished houses, lots for sale, and railway outworks
> Seems re-accepted, resumed . . .
> ('The Bothie of Tober-na-Vuolich')

> Thou shalt have one God only; who
> Would be at the expense of two? . . .
> Thou shalt not kill; but needst not strive
> Officiously to keep alive.
> ('The Latest Decalogue')

> Tibur is beautiful too, and the orchard slopes, and the Anio
> Falling, falling yet, to the ancient lyrical cadence.
> ('Amours de Voyage')

Many of the qualities most distinctive of Clough's work are suggested here: he assumed that the familiar details of Victorian daily life could be valid material for poetry; he used ironic wit and epigram for his most serious purposes, and managed it with adroit sharpness; he extracted lyricism from the sober ordinariness of language, and manipulated the cadences of conversational speech so as to achieve an apparently casual, understated eloquence. All these qualities are typical of Clough, but hardly typical of Victorian poetry.

They make his work unorthodox, inventive, sophisticated and self-conscious. Experiment and strong intelligence mark all that he wrote. One cannot claim that he is a major poet; but his unusual and individual achievement makes him among the most exciting and rewarding of Victorian minor poets.

The 1869 volume of Clough's poetry was reprinted fourteen times before the end of Victoria's reign; but in the twentieth century interest in his work declined. Perhaps Clough did not live long enough to achieve the status of a Great Victorian: he was born in 1819 and died in 1861, when he was only 42. He achieved little in public life, a failure constantly regretted by his friends, who had expected much. His life is nevertheless full of interest. His formative experiences were those of many mid-nineteenth century intellectuals, but he responded to them with exceptional sensitivity. These experiences are germane to an understanding of his poetry and of his surprising eclipse.

The first important phase in Clough's life began in 1829, when he went to Rugby School. Until this time his life had been unusual; his father, a moderately wealthy middle class cotton merchant, had moved from Liverpool to Charleston in the United States when Clough was only four, and Clough did not return to England until 1828. Yet neither Charleston nor his family were important influences; from the time he went to Rugby until his entry to Balliol College, Oxford, in 1837, he was dominated by Dr. Thomas Arnold, the Headmaster. 'This was practically the end of Arthur's childhood', his sister said, of Clough's return to England; justifiably, for after this he was forced to develop precociously under the pressure of the moral and intellectual responsibilities Rugby imposed on him. The discipline of his Rugby training, and the strain he experienced in acquiring it, affected him throughout his life.

Dr. Arnold, whose ideas were to revolutionise the English public school system, found Clough an ideal pupil not only for his academic brilliance, but because he was responsive to the new concepts of boarding-school life which Arnold introduced at Rugby. Clough, with his almost obsessive loyalty to the place, and his efforts, especially in the senior form, to be a moral example to the rest of the school, was an illustration of Arnold's belief that education and moral training were inseparable. Even Clough's early letters are full of self-important piety redolent of Rugby's earnestness— 'Here is a bit of a hymn for you Georgy', he wrote in a P.S. to his younger brother. By the time he was in the senior form he spoke about the school with intense reverence.

> 'I verily believe my whole being is regularly soaked through with the wishing and hoping and striving to do the school good...'
> (20 January, 1836. *Correspondence of A. H. Clough*, Vol. I, p. 35).

Clough never lost the moral scrupulousness fundamental to a Rugby training, even though in the ten years after leaving the school he rejected almost all the particular intellectual positions he had held so unquestioningly while there. Like so many mid-nineteenth century intellectuals, he went through a crisis in religious belief and a period of intense disillusionment with the values of his society. In the long poems written during this time, *The Bothie of Tober-na-Vuolich* (1848), *Amours de Voyage* (1849) and *Dipsychus* (1849-50), the evidence of mental and emotional strain is increasingly obvious.

Clough's period of anxiety began when he was plunged into the theological controversy of the Oxford or Tractarian Movement which was at its height at the time he went up to Oxford in 1837. Dr. Arnold was bitterly opposed to the ideas of John Henry Newman, the leader of the Oxford Movement (which attempted to bring the Anglican Church closer to the Catholic tradition, emphasising accordingly the authority of the Church and the importance of dogma, rather than the Protestant ideas of the responsibility of the individual conscience and private judgement in spiritual matters), and Clough was drawn into the controversy 'like a straw drawn up the draught of a chimney'. The effect of this intensive intellectual upheaval and preoccupation with fundamental religious questions was eventually to undermine *all* his beliefs. To the end of his life Clough felt the need, a need made more acute by his sensitive Rugby conscience, to analyse and re-think every position, in any sphere, religious, political or social. In religion this habit was particularly strong. In his essay on Clough, Walter Bagehot, who knew him, described his temperament in this way: 'If you offer them any known religion they 'won't have that'; if you offer them no religion they will not have that either; if you ask them to accept a new and as yet unrecognised religion, they altogether refuse to do so. They seem not only to believe in an 'unknown God', but in a God whom no man can ever know.' (*Literary Studies*, 1879, Vol. II). Clough's academic achievement also suffered from the distractions of theology, and he did not get the First Class degree expected of him. ('I have failed', he said dramatically to Dr. Arnold after walking from Oxford to Rugby on this occasion). He redeemed himself, however, by winning a fellowship to Oriel College in 1842.

Clough's time at Oxford was not happy; towards the end of his undergraduate career, his father's business began to fail; in June, 1842, Dr. Arnold died; his brother George and his father died shortly afterwards, and in October, 1848, he voluntarily ended his term at Oxford by resigning his fellowship on the grounds that he could no longer make the subscription to the Thirty Nine Articles required by University Statutes. Oxford, nevertheless, was a time of freedom in comparison with his later experiences. At Oxford, he consolidated a lasting friendship with Thomas and Matthew Arnold (particularly with Matthew, the poet), sons of Dr. Arnold. He was an active member of the Decade, an intimate debating club, and in the long vacations went on reading parties to the Lake District or Scotland. These carefree occasions gave him material for his first long poem, *The Bothie of Tober-na-Vuolich* (1848).

After he left Oxford, Clough's life was unsettled until he

married Blanche Smith, a cousin of Florence Nightingale, in 1854. He spent a brief and lonely time in London from 1849 to 1852 where he was in charge of University Hall, a residential Hall for students of University College, London. This period was the nadir of his life. 'He shut himself up and went through his life in silence', his wife wrote of him. Finally, he left University Hall because of difficulties with the authorities over religious observance there, and emigrated to America in 1852, intending to live by writing and teaching at Cambridge, Massachusetts. This was not easy (his largest commission was the drudging task of revising that translation of Plutarch's 'Lives', known as Dryden's) so he returned to England in 1853, and his friends found him a minor post in the Education Office. This post enabled him to marry, but even now he was overwhelmed by work, and with astonishing selflessness he voluntarily increased the strain on his health by assisting his exacting cousin, Florence Nightingale, in her charitable work. Travel abroad in the last year of his life did not restore his health, and he died in Florence in 1861.

The detailed record of Clough's life might at first suggest that he was dogged by misfortune. Yet in spite of the considerable information that exists, and Clough's extensive correspondence, it is difficult to be certain that he was radically damaged by his misfortunes, for his personality is an enigma. His letters, for instance, are in the main so impersonal and toneless that disappointingly little emerges from them (he is exceptionally evasive, for example, about the true nature of his religious problems, and even his love letters are outstanding only for their uncompromising reserve). Though there are letters to a great number of important literary and intellectual figures—Matthew Arnold, Carlyle, Emerson, Froude, Charles Eliot Norton, Jowett, Kingsley—it is difficult to deduce from them why he should have been so highly respected by these men. Even his contemporaries were puzzled by him. This description by Thomas Arnold is hardly informative. It is hesitant, as if

Arnold were aware that he had not completely understood Clough's personality:

> His clear black eyes, under a broad, full and lofty forehead, were often partly closed as if through the pressure of thought; but when the problem occupying him was solved a glorious flash would break from his eyes, expressive of an inner joy and sudden illumination . . . His mouth was beautifully formed, but both it and the chin were characterised by some lack of determination and firmness. This deficiency, however, so far as it existed, was harmful only to himself; those who sought his counsel or help found him the wisest of advisers, the steadiest and kindest of friends.
>
> (Thomas Arnold, *The Nineteenth Century*, 1898).

In the absence of convincing accounts of Clough's personality, conjecture is inevitable. Until recently, the picture of him has been unfortunate and over-simplified, and this may well have discouraged the reading of his poetry. He has been caricatured as the first and quint-essential product of the English public school system (for example, by Lytton Strachey in *Eminent Victorians*); certainly to be mentioned in *Tom Brown's Schooldays*, that naively pious schoolboys' epic of Rugby life under Dr. Arnold, as 'our own Rugby poet', is almost enough to justify such a picture. Alternatively, critics have followed the account of Clough presented in 'Thyrsis', Matthew Arnold's elegy on him. 'Thyrsis', while epitomising Clough as the Victorian intellectual defeated by the dilemmas of his generation, has been far too influential:

> Some life of men unblest
> He knew, which made him droop, and fill'd his head.
> He went; his piping took a troubled sound
> Of storms that rage outside our happy ground;
> He could not wait their passing, he is dead.

'Thyrsis', as even Arnold admitted, is a highly selective account of Clough. Yet his portrait of Clough as the poet of a kind of low seriousness, radically unsettled by anxiety, nagging inconclusively at intellectual problems, has prevailed. Arnold's criticisms have some relevance but they are exaggerated; the neurotic Clough of 'Thyrsis' needs to be modified. Fortunately, this corrective is to be found in an analysis of Clough's poetry by his contemporary, R. H. Hutton. Hutton usefully compares Clough's poetry with that of Matthew Arnold. He recognises that Clough could be over-introspective, but:

> With all his intellectual precision, there is a something of the boyishness, of the simplicity, of the vascular Saxon breadth of Chaucer's poetry in Clough . . . There are both flesh and spirit, as well as emotion and speculation . . . Clough's is the tenderness of earthly sympathy . . . Both [Arnold and Clough] fill half their poems with the most subtle intellectual meditations; but Clough leaves the problems he touches on all but where they were, re-proaching himself for mooning over them so long . . . Finally, when they both reach their highest poetical point, Mr. Arnold is found painting lucidly in a region of pure and exquisite sentiment, Clough singing a sort of paean of buoyant and exultant strength.
> (*Theological and Literary Essays* (1877), Vol. II, p. 256.)

The 'buoyant and exultant strength' described by Hutton has to be constantly invoked to balance the melancholy threnody of *Thyrsis*, for Clough's poetry has firmly positive qualities; it is at once sensitive and sturdy; a strong poetry, permeated with humane objectivity and realism. It is often broadly humorous, brilliantly witty and ironic.

An examination of two of Clough's poems, 'O Land of Empire, art and love!' and 'Say not the struggle nought availeth' will show how assessments of Clough's work as widely apart as those of Arnold and Hutton were possible. It will also serve as an introduction to a general discussion of his work.

(ii) TWO POEMS

'O land of Empire, art and love!' is ostensibly a satire on over-delicacy, but the purpose of the satire is to develop by implication a social theory of art which is deliberately unsentimental and anti-romantic, and which, as will become clear, defends the whole range and subject matter of Clough's poetry. The opening at once establishes the poet's firm common sense and lack of squeamishness. With uninhibited irony, it satirises the uneasy English tourist in Italy, who is alarmed to find that his aesthetic enjoyment of Italian art and culture is spoiled by the squalor of their setting. Clough mocks the tourist's accents:

> Yet, boy, that nuisance why commit
> On this Corinthian column? . . .
> . . . Are these the fixed condition
> On which may Northern pilgrim come
> To imbibe thine ether-air, and sum
> Thy store of old tradition?
> Must we be chill, if clean, and stand
> Foot-deep in dirt in classic land?

As the poem proceeds, the Corinthian column described in the introduction is seen to be the symbol for a work of art, and the physical squalor represents the whole life— sordid and crude as well as refined—of the society which produces a work of art. By using a further analogy between art and a growing flower (thereby bringing in the ideas of vitality and nourishment), Clough makes it clear that art and society must have a symbiotic relation one with another. A healthy art can develop only when it draws upon the whole life of its environment, just as a flower draws upon the earth.

> From homely roots unseen below . . .
> The stem that bears the etherial flower
> Derives that emanative power;
> From mixtures fetid foul and sour
> Draws juices that those petals fill.

Matthew Arnold was to say that poetry is 'at bottom a criticism of life'. In this poem Clough forestalled him and went even further by saying that poetry is primarily a criticism of *everyday* life and society also. It must accept the whole of life, and be firmly related to the solid facts of day-to-day existence. When in 1853 he wrote his *Review of some poems by Alexander Smith and Matthew Arnold*, Clough urgently demanded a new realism, a poetry dealing 'with general wants, ordinary feelings, the obvious rather than the rare facts of human nature', and with 'positive matters of fact'. His own poetry fulfils these demands. In the poetic form particularly suited to describing the domestic affairs of everyday life, the verse novel, he dealt sanely and frankly with love, sex, personal relations. In his poems appear the 'obvious' surroundings and situations of contemporary life: reading parties in Scotland (*The Bothie*), tourism in Europe (*Amours de Voyage*). His theory plainly committed him to write of contemporary problems—social, political and religious—and accordingly he wrote of the siege of Rome in 1849, Chartist ideas, equality, the relation of rich and poor, Strauss and German Biblical criticism. Arnold was particularly disturbed by Clough's willingness to discuss contemporary problems because he felt that it would increase the tendency to morbid intellectuality which, as 'Thyrsis' shows, he considered the flaw of his poetry; but Clough's theory was based on a firm and realistic acceptance of things. It is not surprising that in the review just quoted, he stated a preference for the 'real flesh and blood' of the minor poet, Alexander Smith, in comparison with the fastidiousnes of his friend Matthew Arnold.

'Say not the struggle nought availeth' is Clough's most famous poem.

> Say not the struggle nought availeth,
>   The labour and the wounds are vain,
> The enemy faints not, nor faileth,
>   And as things have been, things remain.
>
> If hopes were dupes, fears may be liars;
>   It may be, in yon smoke concealed,
> Your comrades chase e'en now the fliers,
>   And, but for you, possess the field.

For while the tired waves, vainly breaking,
  Seem here no painful inch to gain,
Far back through creeks and inlets making
  Came, silent, flooding in, the main,

And not by eastern windows only,
  When daylight comes, comes in the light,
In front the sun climbs slow, how slowly,
  But westward, look, the land is bright.

The rejection of defeatism is Clough's most insistent theme. For all his commitment to facts, he was determined never to be defeated by them. The old, well-worn metaphor of battle could easily lead to facile optimism and superficial heroics, but there are none here. Instead, with a peculiarly firm diffidence, he states that fear, just as much as hope, can be deceptive. The very structure of the lines reflects an empirical balance in the thought and precludes attitudinising—'If hopes were dupes, fears may be liars'. 'Say not' is Clough's celebration of a heroic ideal, and yet is rooted in common sense reality. Its strength is that it holds the two moods in equipoise. There is a tension between the sense of achievement, and certain triumph, and the weariness, of dogged, tired effort—'For while the tired waves, vainly breaking . . .' The emotional force of this image is just prevented from dominating the whole poem. It does not counteract the equally powerful rejection of defeat.

This finely adjusted balance is not always achieved in Clough's poetry, and therefore the criticisms in 'Thyrsis', over-stated as they are, cannot altogether be displaced by Hutton's 'buoyant and exultant strength'. Bagehot felt that Dr. Arnold's pupils suffered from 'a fatigued way of looking at great subjects'; certainly, some poems ('Easter Day II' among the short poems, and *Dipsychus* among the long poems), state the intellectual meaning that it is worth 'going on', and yet the general mood of the poem suggests that it is not.

The order in which Clough wrote his poems is not the

order in which they were published. Therefore, before discussing *Ambarvalia*, his earliest work, it is convenient to give a brief chronology in order of publication (omitting the occasional prose pieces, the most important of which were published in *Poems and Prose Remains of A. H. Clough*, 1869, and which are only of relevance in so far as they bear upon his poetry). *The Bothie of Tober-na-Vuolich* appeared in 1848. *Ambarvalia*, a joint production of Clough and Thomas Burbidge*, was published in 1849, though the poems in it were written before *The Bothie*. *Amours de Voyage* first appeared in *The Boston Atlantic Monthly* in 1858, though it was written during 1849. *Dispychus*, published posthumously in 1865, belongs to the same period of composition as *Amours de Voyage*. *Mari Magno*, Clough's last poem, a succession of brief, linked narratives, was composed in 1861 and first appeared in a cut version in 1862. There are a number of shorter poems, and the unfinished *Mystery of the Fall*, belonging to the same period as *Amours de Voyage* and *Dipsychus*.

II AMBARVALIA, 1849

'Why should I say I see the things I see not?'

The title of this volume of poems, *Ambarvalia*, refers to the annual festival in ancient Rome during which the fields and boundaries were purified. It seems to have been chosen as a gesture of modesty, for the festival had homely, agricultural associations. Yet Clough's contributions to the volume have none of the parochialism the title was meant to imply. In comparison with Burbidge's poems, Clough's (written for the most part during his time at Oxford) have an intellectual grip and maturity which are unusual. Burbidge's pieces are capable enough—mild, gentlemanly productions, carefully worked out and sincerely felt—but

---

* Thomas Burbidge (1816-92), was a poet and clergyman. Clough's friendship with him began at Rugby School.

Clough's are imaginatively and intellectually superior because they possess that 'buoyant and exultant strength' which was with him from the beginning.

> Beside me—in the car—she sat,
>   She spake not, no, nor looked at me:
> From her to me, from me to her,
>   What passed so subtly stealthily? . . .
>
>   Yet owned we, fused in one,
>   The Power which e'en in stones and earths
> By blind elections felt, in forms
>   Organic breeds to myriad births;
> By lichen small on granite wall
>   Approved, its faintest feeblest stir
> Slow-spreading, strengthening long, at last
>   Vibrated full in me and her.
>   ('Natura Naturans')

There is an exhilarating response here to those ordinary facts of human life which were already important to Clough. The poet simply meets a girl on a train. With joyful frankness Clough celebrates the physical awareness between them, and then, in a sudden and imaginative enlargement of vision, he shows that the experience gave him insight into the significance of evolution. The slow generation of species culminated in human love and love is the energy working in creation. The muscular strength of the alliteration conveys a sense of fecundity.

> Flashed flickering forth fantastic flies,
>   Big bees their burly bodies swung . . .
> The leopard lithe in Indian glade,
> And dolphin, brightening tropic seas,
>   In us were living, leapt and played.

All the poems in *Ambarvalia* manifest Clough's strength; his expressions of moral responsibility have a firmness, a quiet integrity and eloquence. There is the sober, urgent dignity of 'Qui laborat orat', in which Clough says that genuine prayer expresses itself as action in practical life, an early statement of an habitual theme. Or there is the poised gravity of 'Qua cursum ventus':

> To veer, how vain! On, onward strain,
>> Brave barks! In light, in darkness too,
> Through winds and tides one compass guides—
>> To that, and your own selves, be true.

Something more distinguishes Clough's poems—a theme. The aggressive 'Why should I say I see the things I see not?' is a key line. The poems defend intellectual honesty; implicitly or explicitly they claim the right to question, the right to be sceptical, demanding enquiry and analysis in every sphere. There is the iconoclastic poem on duty, where Clough attacks social convention because it restricts intellectual and moral freedom:

> Ready money of affection
>> Pay, whoever drew the bill.
> With the form conforming duly,
> Senseless what it meaneth truly,
> Go to church—the world require you,
>> To balls—the world require you too ...
> Duty—'tis to take on trust
>> What things are good, and right, and just.
>>>> ('Duty—that's to say complying')

In another poem on religion he examines the possibility of belief or non-belief alike with conscientious distrust, and reiterates an honest scepticism rather than the honest doubt which Tennyson later professed in *In Memoriam*:

> Receive it not, but leave it not,
>> And wait it out, O Man!
>>>> ('When Israel came out of Egypt')

In this constant intellectual analysis, Clough transferred his Rugby scrupulousness to all areas of experience. He once wrote that he wanted to escape 'the vortex of Philosophism' at Oxford, yet 'Philosophism' is germane to these poems. In the more mature longer poems he turned it to further artistic advantage, and evolved a highly successful technique for presenting 'Philosophism' in verse.

III THE LONGER POEMS:

The Bothie of Tober-na-Vuolich
Amours de Voyage
Dipsychus

(i) 'Myself my own experiment'

'. . . but you know you are a mere d — d depth hunter in poetry', Arnold wrote to Clough in a letter of 24 May 1848, shortly before the publication of *The Bothie*. He was objecting to the predominance of 'thinking aloud' in Clough's poetry, but in accusing him of trying to 'solve the universe', and in interpreting this as a sign of weakness, Arnold underrated Clough's self-consciousness and intelligence, failing to grasp that in these poems, reasoning is not only a procedure but a theme. All these poems, though they otherwise differ, have a common theme—that of the intellectual temperament itself.

In *Ambarvalia* Clough insisted on the primacy of analysis and enquiry but he understood its dangers. He early recognised his own tendency to what he called in a letter of 26 August, 1837, 'double-mindedness', a faculty for analysing problems so minutely and fairly that what started as a discipline in empirical honesty ended as vacillating inconclusiveness. Asserting his pragmatic commitment to 'positive matters of fact' in the long poems, he satirised any kind of gratuitous theorising (whether it took the form of abstract speculation or introspection). The long poems are brilliant studies in the psychology of intellectuals.

Clough regarded the over-analytic temperament seriously

enough to make it the crux of the unfinished *Mystery of the Fall* where it is the salient characteristic of fallen man. Adam exults in reasoning and self-analysis because the 'curious seething process' of introspection makes him intellectually autonomous—'myself my own experiment'. But Eve condemns the interminable 'thinkings and cross-thinkings' which began with self-consciousness. These 'thinkings and cross-thinkings' are dramatised in the long poems. The hero of *The Bothie*, Philip, is the victim of his own over-impulsive theorising. Claude, the hero of *Amours de Voyage*, is betrayed by his fastidious introspections, and the hero of *Dipsychus* has an almost pathological conscientiousness.

Though Arnold and Clough seem to be diametrically opposed as to poetic principles, their diagnosis of the vitiating intellectual habit of the nineteenth century was the same; they agree that this habit was a morbid 'dialogue of the mind with itself', as Arnold called it in the preface to his own poems of 1853. Arnold tried to eradicate it altogether from his poetry; Clough deliberately explored it. In doing so he avoided morbidity (two of the poems are straightforward comedies) by means of presenting the psychology of the analytic mind dramatically; '. . . it is both critically best and morally safest to dramaticize [sic] your feelings where they are of private personal character', he wrote in a letter of 7 July, 1838, early in his poetic career. In the three long poems, Clough greatly developed the 'dramaticizing' method, and the dramaticizing technique creates the effect of impersonal, objective presentation. Further, the dramatic presentation allows him to pack these poems with energy and life because his intellectuals soliloquise in a concrete, vividly delineated environment, surrounded by characters as much individualised as themselves. The sense of locality is so strong that the characters never become detached from their contexts. In *Amours de Voyage* ,which is set in Rome, the topography of Rome and its surroundings is never allowed to become indistinct:

Ye, too, Ye marvellous Twain, that erect on Monte Cavallo
Stand by your rearing steeds in the grace of your
motionless movement,
Stand with your upstretched arms and tranquil
regardant faces,
Stand as instinct with life in the might of immutable
manhood,—

These long poems are Clough's major achievement and
culminate in the *tour de force* of *Dipsychus*, where Clough
treated the theme of the intellectual with more seriousness,
if with more pessimism, than in the other poems.

(ii)   *Intellectuals ebullient*

The Bothie of Tober-na-Vuolich and *Amours de Voyage*

These two poems, both verse novels written in hexameters, are predominantly comic studies of intellectuals.
The Bothie is a mock heroic account of an undergraduate
reading party or vacation study group in Scotland. Philip,
the hero, is full of unrealistic radical and egalitarian ideas
which lead him particularly to sentimentalise working class
women. Slipping away from his companions while on a
walking tour, he has an eminently rash flirtation with a
servant girl, Katie. His disappointment over this affair
drives him to the other extreme, and he has an equally
unsuccessful flirtation with an heiress, Lady Maria. His
friends and tutor hear rumours of his activities with suspense
and puzzlement shared by the reader. Finally, he falls
genuinely in love with Elspie, a poor Highland girl, daughter
of the owner of the 'bothie' or hut, named in the title of
the poem. As he achieves emotional maturity and a sense
of responsibility in personal relationships, so he begins to
hold his political ideas with more realism. The two processes
are interdependent.

Amours de Voyage is in letter form. Claude, the hero,
happens to visit Rome during Mazzini's defence of the

Roman republic when the French besieged Rome in 1849. He is thrown into the company of the Trevellyns, an English family also travelling. He loses the opportunity to propose to their daughter, Mary, who loves him, by examining his state of mind so lengthily that she leaves Rome before he has completed his self-analysis. Claude can make up his mind about nothing; 'Il doutait de tout, même de l'amour', runs one of the epigraphs to the poem.

In each poem the intellectual and his characteristics emerge fully from the narrative. Wit is an almost obligatory part of the intellectual's equipment, and Clough exploited the intellectual's wit and wrote from within its own terms— its jokes, epigrams, aphorisms, its ebullient delight in sheer sophisticated cleverness, or its effervescent, extravagant indulgence in undergraduate humour. The humour of these poems is always the humour of the educated. Clough understood the humour of the intellectual mentality so well that he reproduced with remarkable authenticity the educated voice, speaking from the intellectual's exclusive world of assured knowledge, and easy, almost negligent intelligence. When the undergraduates of *The Bothie* decide to abandon their studies temporarily, they dismiss the classics with an absurd, exhilarated mock-rhetorical apostrophe which only a knowledge of the classics could have allowed them to make:

> Slumber in Liddell-and-Scott, O musical chaff
> of old Athens,
> Dishes, and fishes, bird, beast, and sesquipedalian
> blackguard!
> Sleep, weary ghosts, be at peace and abide in your lexicon-
> limbo!

Claude, the hero of *Amours de Voyage*, analyses Italian art and culture in knowledgeable, elegant arabesques of wit as he wanders in Rome. 'Rome disappoints me much', he says. '*Rubbishy* seems the word that most exactly would suit it.'

What do I find in the Forum? An archway and
                      two or three pillars.
Well, but St. Peter's? Alas, Bernini has filled
                      it with sculpture!
... Yet of solidity much, but of splendour little is
                      extant:
'Brickwork I found thee, and marble I left thee!'
                      their Emperor vaunted:
'Marble I thought thee, and brickwork I find thee!'
                      the Tourist may answer.

All the freedom of comment, irreverence and iconoclastic
allusion in these poems is achieved by exploiting the voice
of the intellectual.

The dramatic situations of *The Bothie* and *Amours de
Voyage* are the same—the intellectual in love—and yet the
two poems are very different. *The Bothie*, despite its searching criticism of Philip's ideals, is a young man's idyll,
while *Amours de Voyage* is a mature and highly finished
satire. Accordingly, in *Amours de Voyage* elegant verbal
sharpness supersedes the boisterous mock-heroic verse of
The Bothie. Yet the boisterousness of *The Bothie* gives the
poem its distinctive 'buoyant and exultant' energy. Clough
parodies epic description with exuberance; he makes one
young man dress for dinner in the 'waistcoat work of a
lady', and another in a 'shirt as of crochet of women' as if
they were elaborately arming for battle. The best swimmer
in the company becomes heroically 'the Glory of Headers'.
And yet this mocking syntax, which sounds like a pedanti-
cally literal translation, moves easily into the lyrical phrasing
of 'perfection of water' when Clough describes the pool
used by the group for bathing:

              where beads of foam uprising
        Mingle their clouds of white with the delicate hue of the
                                      stillness.

Clough never allows the poem to lose buoyancy. The

grave advice of the young man's tutor, Adam, is juxtaposed
with a flippant discussion of women put into the terminology
of Gothic architecture—the 'sculliony stumpy-columnar',
the 'Modern-Florid, modern-fine-lady'. When Philip
laments over Katie, feeling that he has deserted her too
brutally, his sad reiterations—'Would I were dead, I keep saying, that so I could go and uphold her!'—are followed immediately by a gay account of a Highland reel, 'swinging
and flinging, and stamping and tramping, and grasping
and clasping'.

The gaiety of *The Bothie*, is mitigated in *Amours de Voyage*;
here Clough presents the fastidious introspections of Claude,
the over-selfconscious intellectual, with particularly cutting
satire. Claude is so intellectually scrupulous, witty, sensitive,
cleverly cruel, that he reduces all experience to bathos.
When he exclaims 'Hang this thinking!', he inadvertently
defines his own weakness. His habit of analysis is a defence
against what he calls 'the factitious'. He is so afraid of the
factitious that he cannot believe even in his own emotion.

'I am in love, you say: I do not think so, exactly.'

The line—a lingering half-denial followed by a half-
retraction—is the epitome of equivocation. In the comedy
of the statement, with its scrupulous phraseology, and the
final outrageous pseudo-precision of 'exactly', Clough does
not disguise Claude's chronic inability to commit himself.

As a self-conscious study in self-consciousness, *Amours
de Voyage* is a kind of nineteenth century '*Love song of
J. Alfred Prufrock*'. In both poems, the mixture of wit and
poignancy, comedy and pain, comes from the protagonist's
never quite successful attempt to control emotions by re-
ducing their importance. Claude's intellectual posturings
and defensive detachment are shared by Eliot's hero. The
protagonists of both poems have a faculty for dismissing
themselves with self-deprecating irony, a sort of super-
cilious verbal shrug.

> I grow old . . . I grow old . . .
> I shall wear the bottoms of my trousers rolled.
> ('Prufrock')
> After all, perhaps there was something factitious about it;
> I have had pain, it is true; have wept; and so have the actors.

Amours de Voyage, however cutting its satire, is not a harsh poem. It is constantly lightened by the brilliant verbal extravagance of Claude himself: 'After endeavouring idly to minister balm to the trembling Quinquagenarian fears of two lone British spinsters'—thus he describes his gallantry during the siege. Clough broadens the poem by presenting other characters beside Claude, and by treating Mary's feelings with genuine sympathy. Mary's typically Victorian family, naive middle class tourists who create their unmistakeably British ethos with complete assurance wherever they go, are refreshingly normal. Her sister, Georgina, engaged to the 'tender domestic' Vernon, is particularly appealing, chattering her way through Rome with artless superficiality:

> Rome is a wonderful place . . .
> Not very gay, however; the English are mostly
> at Naples;
> There are the A.'s, we hear, and most of the W. party.

Mary herself ends the poem, determining to forget Claude in sad but sane resignation. 'You have heard nothing [of Claude]; of course, I know you can have heard nothing', she writes to a friend. Her resignation puts the action of the poem in proportion, a proportion provided also by the short lyrics which head each canto. These, recalling in warm and tender lyricism the ancient Rome of gods and heroes which 'Lives in the exquisite grace of column disjointed and single', are set against the tensions of the siege, and the emotional problems of the central characters.

> Over the great windy waters, and over the clear-crested
> summits,
> Unto the sun and the sky, and unto the perfecter
> earth,
> Come, let us go,—to a land wherein gods of the old time
> wandered,
> Where every breath even now changes to ether
> divine.

(iii)   *Dipsychus—The intellectual agonistes*

Dipsychus is set in Venice, and consists of a series of soliloquies and dialogues between Dipsychus and a character designated as 'Spirit', as they wander through Venice. 'Dipsychus' translated means 'double-minded', and the double-mindedness of Dipsychus is of the moral sort. 'Now the over-tender conscience will, of course, exaggerate the wickedness of the world', Clough wrote in the Epilogue to *Dipsychus*. Dipsychus is divided against himself because his moral scruples prevent him from deciding on any course of action in the morally degenerate society (as he interprets it) in which he lives. The Spirit, always in opposition to Dipsychus, represents this materialist society, the society of mid-nineteenth century Europe.

'I could have gone cracked . . .' was Clough's comment on his state of mind during the time he composed *Dipsychus*, and the poem has none of the free assurance behind *The Bothie* and *Amours de Voyage*. Its equivalent to their wit is a tone of corroding mockery and tragic cynicism:

> I dreamt a dream; till morning light
> A bell rang in my head all night,
> Tinkling and tinkling first, and then
> Tolling; and tinkling; tolling again.
> So brisk and gay, and then so slow!
> O joy, and terror! mirth, and woe!
> Ting, ting, there is no God; ting, ting—
> Dong, there is no God; dong,
> There is no God; dong, dong!

Dipsychus is a study of the mental and spiritual crisis of the contemporary Victorian intellectual, and voices the sense of loss—loss of belief, loss of confidence in the values of society—which fills so much of Victorian poetry. The intellectual's dilemma in *Dipsychus* is that his values run counter to the values of society so that he is in moral isolation. He is able to diagnose but not to remedy the limitations of his society and the predicament is demoralising. Since it has this wide reference, *Dipsychus* is more ambitious than the other long poems, though it was never finished.

The opposition between the intellectual and his society is displayed by means of counterpoint. Throughout the poem Dipsychus's despair of society and the Spirit's cynical acceptance of it create a counterpoint of moods and attitudes. Deep emotion alternates with callousness, just as in the elegy quoted above, which alternates lightness and resonance

> 'Ting, ting, there is no God; ting, ting—
> Dong, there is no God, dong . . .'

Clough allows the Spirit to voice among other things the materialist attitudes which he particularly wanted to attack; and the Spirit, a cheerfully insensitive philistine, subjects all major questions—sex, class, religion—to a coarse irony:

> . . . Once in a fortnight say, by lucky chance
> Of happier-tempered coffee, gain (Great Heaven!)
> A pious rapture.
>
> Why as to feelings of devotion—
> I interdict all vague emotion.
>
> They may talk as they please about what they call pelf,
> And how one ought never to think of one's self,
> And how pleasures of thought surpass eating and drinking—
> My pleasure of thought is the pleasure of thinking
>   How pleasant it is to have money, heigh ho!
>   How pleasant it is to have money.

This satire is a continuation of Clough's attacks on commercial values begun in *The Bothie* and extended in short poems such as 'In the Great Metropolis', with its savage jig-like refrain 'The devil take the hind most, O!' (Clough was radical enough to be addressed by his friends as 'Citizen Clough'). In *Dipsychus* the satire is deepened and supplemented by the profounder despairing commentary of Dipsychus himself. He cannot share the common sense of the Spirit who will recognize a vague and ill-defined God when distress or trouble force him to take refuge in belief.

> And almost every one when age,
> Disease, or sorrows strike him,
> Inclines to think there is a God,
> Or something very like Him.

Dipsychus feels too intensely the loss of firm Christian morality and religious feeling.

> O pretty girl who trippest along,
> Come to my bed—it isn't wrong.
> Uncork the bottle, sing the song!
> Ting, ting a ding: dong, dong.
> Wine has dregs; the song an end;
> A silly girl is a poor friend
> And age and weakness who shall mend?
> Dong, there is no God; Dong!

Dipsychus's statements have a dramatic immediacy because of their directly topical implications, yet their seriousness gives the poem more than topical relevance.

The antagonism between Dipsychus and the Spirit represents more than the antagonism between the intellectual and his society. The satire in the poem has a double focus, and the opposition between the two characters serves a further purpose. It represents the conflict of an over-sensitive conscience (Dipsychus might have been a product of Dr. Arnold's Rugby) with instinct and impulse, the animal side of man which Dipsychus regards with unnecessary dread and timidity. In this sense the poem is a dialogue between soul and body, taking place within Dipsychus himself. However superficial the Spirit's morality, he has the reasonableness of the natural man eminently lacking in Dipsychus. His flippant Gilbertian rhymes and neat satiric couplets embody some precise and acute comment, and he speaks the most energetic verse in the poem:

> These juicy meats, this flashing wine,
> May be an unreal mere appearance;
> Only—for my inside, in fine,
> They have a singular coherence.
>
> This lovely creature's glowing charms
> Are gross illusion, I don't doubt that;
> But when I pressed her in my arms
> I somehow didn't think about that.
>
>   *   *   *
>
> Thus life we see is wondrous odd,
> And so, we argue, may be God.
> At any rate, this rationalistic
> Half-puritano—semitheistic
> Cross of Neologist and mystic
> Is, of all doctrines, the least reasonable.

The spirit emphasises that Dipsychus makes his problems more acute by being intellectually and morally effete. Fastidiously afraid of being contaminated by the vices of 'the world', he is too much inhibited by moral scruples, as Claude was by intellectual scruples. 'It's all Arnold's doing; he spoilt the public schools', grumbles the supposed uncle of the author who discusses the poem with him in the engaging epilogue to *Dipsychus*. He echoes a friend's criticism of Rugby boys—'They're all so pious'; the situation of Dipsychus makes his comment almost justifiable.

Dipsychus is the only one of Clough's poems to which the criticisms in 'Thyrsis' are applicable. The 'feeling of

depression, the feeling of ennui', which Arnold described
as the dominating mood of his generation are to be found
in *Dipsychus* because it is infused with the self-pity it tries
to objectify. *Dipsychus* opens with a specific reference to an
earlier poem, 'Easter Day', an elegy on the general loss of
Christian morality and religious feeling. The literal occur-
rence of the Resurrection in the past, Clough says there,
is of minor importance compared with the necessity to
practise Christian morality in the present:

> Weep not beside the Tomb
> Ye women . . .
> Go to your homes, your living children tend,
> Your earthly spouses love;
> Set your affections *not* on things above . . .

This shows signs of the influence of Carlyle, whose early
essays, with their doctrine of work ('Do the Duty which lies
nearest to thee.') Clough read enthusiastically as an undergraduate. Clough's confidence in these ideas had lessened by
the time he wrote *Dipsychus*. Perhaps, as Bagehot suggests,
those 'terrible notions of duty' (*Amours de Voyage*) instilled
by Dr. Arnold proved too exhausting. The poem has some
of that drudging weariness which is just controlled in
'Say not'. Though Dipsychus takes up the words of 'Easter
Day' in the opening elegy—'Christ is not risen'—it has
none of the implicit confidence asserted by the resonant
phrasing of 'Easter Day'. In 'Easter Day' Clough rejected
Christian myth but maintained hope in Christian morality
and therefore there is a certain stoical grandeur in his
rejection of the Resurrection, a grandeur lacking in
Dipsychus, in spite of the profoundly elegaic quality of
Dipsychus's laments, and the vigour of the Spirit's verse:

> Through the great sinful streets of Naples as I past,
> With fiercer heat than flamed above my head
> My heart was hot within me; till at last
> My brain was lightened, when my tongue had said

Christ is not risen!

Christ is not risen, no,
He lies and moulders low;
Christ is not risen.
('Easter Day').

(iv) *Clough's allegory of the commonplace in the long poems*

Arnold was too much of a purist fully to appreciate Clough's work. He wished to remove poetry as far as possible from the commonplace—a position exactly the opposite of Clough's. The essentials of poetry, Arnold wrote in 1853 (in the Preface to his own volume of poetry), were 'great actions, calculated powerfully and delightfully to affect what is permanent in the human soul'. The actions of Clough's poems—all local, topical and domestic— seemed to him to fall far short of these essentials. Yet Arnold was led to misread Clough. All Clough's long poems transcend a narrowly contemporary significance. To understand why it is necessary to return again to his emphasis on 'positive matters of fact'; the reiterated theme of those long poems is the importance of the commonplace. They all assert that life has to be lived actively and creatively in and through the commonplace. This is the equivalent of the 'great actions' proposed by Arnold. In Clough's poems the 'permanent' things are the commonplace emotions and activities of ordinary experience and practical life. Taken together, these poems are a protest against the devaluation of ordinary experience and this is the permanently relevant theme of Clough's poetry.

The long poems repeatedly show the fallacy of departing from 'positive matters of fact' (fact is a key word in them), and whatever the subject under discussion—love, religion, social criticism, politics—it is always checked against solid reality. Clough's imaginative perception of the possibilities of ordinary experience shows itself particularly when he uses a group of symbolic situations and images which he relates firmly to the commonplace facts of everyday life—battle, marriage, building, growing things. These gather significance as they are explored in the poems, sometimes appearing as metaphors, or literal situations in the poems may be simultaneously real and allegorical. Battle is one of the most significant symbols, and as in 'Say Not', Clough revivifies this well-worn image by giving it a precise application, particularly in *The Bothie* and *Amours de Voyage*, and exploring it with his customary sanity.

The battle symbol was particularly suitable for Clough's purpose; it implies a practical struggle in exacting circumstances, and he used it to show that the actuality of the commonplace must be accepted with similar action and vigour. Such an acceptance of the facts was to him a great and demanding exercise, and the heroic associations of battle endorse this idea—an idea condensed in 'Say not the struggle nought availeth'. In *The Bothie*, just as in 'Say not', the battle image is used to renounce defeatism. At the end of *The Bothie*, Philip, whose love for Elspie has given him new hopes and a new sense of responsibility, decides to give his social ideals a practical application. He regains vigour and energy, asking 'Where is the battle!'

> O where is the battle!
> Neither battle I see, nor arraying, nor king in Israel,
> Only infinite jumble and mess and dislocation,
> Backed by a solemn appeal, 'For God's sake do
> not stir, there!'

The decision to fight the 'infinite jumble' of society is supported by two metaphors of hope, the tide turning, and daylight gradually illuminating a drab town.

> As at return of tide the total weight of ocean,
> Drawn by moon and sun from Labrador and Greenland,
> Sets-in amain, in the open space betwixt Mull and Scarba,

> Heaving, swelling, spreading, the might of the mighty
> > Atlantic;
> There into cranny and slit of the rocky, cavernous bottom
> Settles down, and with dimples huge the smooth sea-surface
> Eddies, coils, and whirls; by dangerous Corryvreckan:
> So in my soul of souls through its cells and secret recesses,
> Comes back, swelling and spreading, the old democratic
> > fervour.
> But as the light of day enters some populous city,
> Shaming away, ere it come, by the chilly day-streak signal,
> High and low, the misusers of night, shaming out the
> > gas lamps—
> All the great empty streets are flooded with broadening
> > clearness,
> Which, withal, by inscrutable simultaneous access
> Permeates far and pierces to the very cellars lying in
> Narrow high back-lane, and court, and alley of alleys . . .
> —Such—in me, and to me, and on me the love of Elspie!

This passage, where the hexameters gather a magnificent energy, is one of the finest sustained pieces Clough ever wrote. The images of battle, sea and daylight are parallel with those used in 'Say not', and they have identical implications.

In *Amours de Voyage* the actual battle during the siege of Rome takes on a symbolic meaning, and it is used to expose Claude's habit of devaluating all important experience, particularly the common experience of falling in love. When Rome is besieged by the French, he asks of the Italians 'Will they fight?' Will he himself fight? 'Am I prepared to lay down my life for the British female?' he asks, wondering whether he will assist the English women during the siege, and the parodying tone immediately reduces an ethical question to one of ironic good manners. By fighting against the French in an unequal struggle, the Italians attempt on the public, social level what Claude fails to attempt on the personal level when he retreats from the responsibilities of his love affair. Claude's literal refusal 'to lay down my life for the British female' is also a metaphorical rejection of effort and action not only in the sphere of personal relationships but in all spheres of experience, a refusal to fight the symbolic battle of *The Bothie* and 'Say not'. The battle in Clough's poetry always stands for commitment to experience and actuality. Clough's battle symbol contrasts sharply with Arnold's. His armies are not the 'ignorant armies' which 'clash by night' of Arnold's 'Dover Beach'.

(v) *'Grotesque' style and 'hurry scurry anapaests'*

Arnold wrote, complaining of Clough's style, of 'A growing sense of the deficiency of the beautiful in your poems' (24 Feb., 1848). He complained thus well before the publication of *Ambarvalia*; when Clough adopted the hexameter he was generally unsympathetic. Much later he described elements of Clough's style as 'grotesque', and Clough's use of the hexameter must have seemed to him gratuitously inelegant.

> On the whole, we conclude the Romans won't do it,
> > and I shan't.
> > > (*Amours de Voyage*)

Certainly, on first inspection the elements of Clough's style seem unpromising; the lines are built up by a simple grammar full of slack construction, relying on long series of unconnected adjectives, and on the simple connective expedient of 'and'; this ramifying grammar supports cumbersome words; the lines abound in repetition. Clough had his own conception of 'the beautiful', resting on the axiom that almost any word or expression, however ordinary or however grotesque, has potential poetic value, just as he recognised that almost any situation is capable of poetic treatment. From this basis he created an idiom of extraordinary sensitivity and expressiveness.

By far his most frequent poetic device is repetition—repetition of words, of phrases, repetition in the form of synonymous expressions. Yet it never becomes monotonous. In the following passage it creates a literal, understated lyricism, emerging unassumingly with sober beauty from the most ordinary details of description and from the most ordinary words:

> . . . where over a ledge of granite
> Into a granite basin the amber torrent descended;
> Beautiful, very, to gaze-in ere plunging; beautiful also,
> Perfect as picture, as vision entrancing that comes to the
> sightless,
> Through the great granite jambs the stream, the glen,
> and the mountain,
> Beautiful, seen by snatches at intervals of dressing,
> Morn after morn, unsought for, recurring;
> (*The Bothie of Tober-na-Vuolich*)

The most controversial element in Clough's poetry is his hexameter. The hexameter is a six stress line which, when it is unrhymed, can be used even more freely than blank verse, and Clough realised that he could create with it a supple line, full of modulations of phrasing. His hexameters are used to achieve informal, naturalistic speech rhythms. They sound casual, yet they demand as much technical skill as the disciplined satiric couplets spoken by the Spirit in *Dipsychus*. In the Prologue to *Dipsychus*, the supposed uncle of the author attacks his nephew's 'hurry scurry anapaests', and objects that there can be 'three or four ways of reading' every line, 'each as good and as much intended as the other'. But the author defends his refusal to keep to the metrical stress of the line and shows that the deviation is deliberate. And this calculated deviation is justified by the verse, for by it Clough achieved subtle shifts of emphasis, pauses, and delicate rhythmic effects. Such flexible irregularities make his hexameter a precise instrument. It can record the fussy volubility of Georgina, Mary Trevellyn's sister, in *Amours de Voyage*:

> Dear, I must really stop, for the carriage, they
>   tell me, is waiting.

Or it can realise the slow movement of pauses and re-commencements as in the cadences of the following line. By its sheer phrasing, lyrically embodying Claude's involuntary enchantment with Mary Trevellyn, it achieves 'the beautiful':

> She goes,—therefore I go; she moves,—I move, not
>   to lose her.

IV. MARI MAGNO—'On the great sea'

Mari Magno, resembling in structure Chaucer's *Canterbury Tales*, is a series of tales told by strangers travelling to America on a liner. The tales themselves are all of travel—in England and Scotland, on the continent, to the colonies. Travel is indeed related to the main theme of *Mari Magno*. All the stories are about love and marriage: the success or failure of personal relations; the physical travel and movement which the characters have to undertake represents the demands of changing experience. Clough used the tales in *Mari Magno* to ask: What is love? Does it work out in experience? How far is it dependent on circumstances? These are the questions behind his examination of adolescent love (The Lawyer's First Tale, The Clergyman's First Tale), love, marriage and sexual infidelity (The Clergyman's Second Tale), love, marriage and class (The Lawyer's Second Tale), love and chance, love and expedience (The American's Tale, The Mate's Story). Clough had also used travel with a semi-symbolic sense in the other poems; in *Amours de Voyage*, for instance, Claude decides to travel to Egypt, and his aimless travel reflects his vacillating temperament. Yet the travel motif is more dominant in *Mari Magno* because the poem is particularly concerned with the challenge of change.

Hutton's remark, 'Clough's is the tenderness of earthly sympathy' is particularly relevant to *Mari Magno*. A realistic tenderness and a kind of humane poignancy are the poem's shaping moods. These moods are not common in the long poems, though they emerge in short lyrics such as 'Les Vaches', a poem at once exquisite and sturdy, the reverie of a peasant girl as she drives the cows home and wonders how she and her lover will stand the test of time:

> Ah dear, and where is he, a year agone
> Who stepped beside and cheered us on and on?
> My sweetheart wanders far away from me,
> In foreign land or o'er a foreign sea.
> Home, Rose, and home, Provence and La Palie.
>
> ... Or shall he find before his term be sped,
> Some comelier maid that he shall wish to wed?
> (Home, Rose, and home, Provence and La Palie,)
> For weary is work, and weary day by day
> To have your comfort miles on miles away.

With the same sensitive realism that underlies 'Les Vaches', Clough writes in *Mari Magno* of adultery, seduction, illegitimacy, the force of sexual desire. *Mari Magno* is distinguished from the other long poems by its subtle treatment of the emotions. This passage in the Clergyman's First Tale, where an adolescent boy first becomes aware of adult feeling, is characteristic of the poem:

> 'Emma', he called,—then knew that he was wrong,
> Knew that her name to him did not belong.
> Half was the colour mounted on her face,
> Her tardy movement had an adult grace.
> Her look and manner proved his feeling true,—
> A child no more, her womanhood she knew.
> Vexed with himself, and shamed, he felt ...
> Something there was that from this date began,
> Within their bloods a common feeling ran.

The new tenderness in *Mari Magno* does not entirely compensate for the loss of other qualities. It is a retrospective poem. Habitual themes and situations reappear—an Oxford don falls in love with a Highland girl, a young man is unable to make up his mind about his feelings—and there is a loss of immediacy in the repetition. *Mari Magno* is deficient in comedy; though the lyric of the *Conducteur* (who cannot put love behind him in spite of middle age) in 'My Tale' is wryly humorous, the ebullient wit and iconoclasm of the early poems is absent. All in all, *Mari Magno* does not equal the achievement of the earlier long poems. Clough abandoned the 'dramaticizing' technique, and the poem lacks the vitality of the other poems because the characters no longer speak for themselves. He replaced the hexameter either with octosyllabic or heroic couplets, and by keeping strictly to the metrical stress he eliminated some of the elements which give life to his verse—variety of cadence, idiomatic tones. The plainness of the language is often flat, without its customary succinctness. It was as if he were determined that no device of style, no image or linguistic detail, should get between the reader and the reality of the human situations he describes. His desire for 'positive matters of fact' defeats the poetry in *Mari Magno* by making it factual.

V. CONCLUSION: *The Janus-poet*

It is difficult to assess Clough's work with any finality because of the paradoxes within it. He is in some ways a precursor of twentieth century poetry, yet some aspects of his work make it possible to discuss him as a poet within the eighteenth century tradition who found himself living in the nineteenth century. He has a special minor place in English poetry since he is a Janus-like poet, both retrospective and revolutionary.

By temperament empirical and pragmatic, eminently concerned with fact, objectivity and common sense,

Clough might seem emotionally and intellectually of the eighteenth century. His poetry is intelligent, witty and satiric; it is concerned with society as well as the poet's individual imagination; it has formal and verbal affinities with eighteenth century poetry. On the other hand, Clough was disturbed by a consciousness of disequilibrium and instability, and these have to be emphasised when he is considered as a precursor of modern poetry.

> . . . I see . . .
> Only infinite jumble and mess and dislocation.

The frustration with which the isolated intellectual views his society is the phenomenon of modern poetry; so is his response to this condition—analysis, the 'dialogue of the mind with itself'—and Clough acknowledged and responded to the modern situation in this way. In content, the inclusiveness and realism he demanded anticipated the modern poetry of the city, the urban and industrial environment; in technique, his hexameter achieved some of the rhythmical freedom of modern verse.

That Clough's poetry can be analysed in two ways points to the complexities of his work, its peculiar blend of sensitive commonsense, sturdiness and sophistication. If these qualities are puzzling, they make for endurance. Clough's work is still important and relevant. He was one of the first poets to write about the intellectual; the searching, buoyant sanity he brought to problems still familiar will always be refreshing. He was one of the few Victorian poets to be witty without writing 'comic' verse, and he is not witty alone but serious without being heavy, moving without being melodramatic. His most enduring quality proves to be what his wife called, rather anxiously, 'honest coarse strength and perception'. Though she added, 'can there not be strength without losing delicacy?', Clough's 'coarse strength' vindicates his poetry by giving it energy. Even Arnold, always Clough's most persistent critic, allowed him on this account the finest praise. Though he was writing about *The Bothie*, his remark applies to a great deal in Clough's work as a whole; it gives the reader, he said, 'the sense of having, within short limits of time, a large portion of human life presented to him, instead of a small portion'.

ARTHUR HUGH CLOUGH

A Select Bibliography

(Place of publication London, unless stated otherwise)

Note:

The bulk of the Clough MSS are in the Bodleian Library, Oxford. They were presented in 1959 by Miss Blanche Athena Clough and Miss Katherine Duff. Other documents are at Balliol College, Oxford, Oriel College, Oxford, and Dr. Williams Library, London. In America there are MSS in the Houghton Library, Harvard University, and some journals deposited with the Honnold Library, University of California. Particulars of Clough's MS notebooks and papers are given in the definitive edition of his POEMS (1951).

Bibliographies:

BIBLIOGRAPHIES OF TWELVE VICTORIAN AUTHORS, by T. G. Ehrsam and R. H. Deily. New York (1936)
—records only books and articles about Clough.
A Supplement by J. G. Fucilla appeared in *Modern Philology*, XXXVII, 1939.
THE VICTORIAN POETS, A Guide to Research: edited by F. E. Faverty. Cambridge, Mass. (1956).
'Prose Works of Clough: A Check List and Calendar.' by W. E. Houghton in the *Bulletin of the New York Public Library*, 64. 1960
—this check-list will form Part 2 of a general bibliography on Clough which is to appear in 1963.

Collected Works:

THE RUGBY MAGAZINE, 2 vols. (1835-7)
—Clough edited six out of the eight issues of the Rugby School magazine. 17 poems and 13 articles by him are signed variously "T.Y.C.", "Z" and "A.V.".

Poems in the *Rugby Magazine* assumed to be Clough's:
'The Poacher of Dead Man's Corner, vol. 1, p.35 (July 1835);
'The Warrior's Last Fight, vol. 1, p.62 (July 1835); 'Count Egmont', vol. 1, p. 160 (October 1835); 'Sonnet I', 'Sonnet 4', vol. 1, p. 173, 175

(October 1835); 'I watched them from the Window', vol. 1, p. 308 (Jan. 1836); 'Song of the Hyperborean Maidens', vol. 1, p. 309 (Jan. 1836); 'To ———, on going to India', vol. 1, p. 320 (April 1836); 'The old man of Athens', vol. 1, p. 399 (April 1836); 'The Exordium of a very long Poem', vol. 1, p. 404 (April 1836); 'Lines', vol. 2, p. 74 (July 1836); 'An Answer to Memory', vol. 2, p. 132 (December 1836); 'An Incident', vol. 2, p. 135 (December 1836); 'Epilogue to the Sonnets' vol. 2, p. 284 (July 1837); 'Verses from the School House', vol. 2, p. 346 (November 1837); 'Rosabel's Dream', vol. 2, p. 361 (November 1837); 'To a Crab Tree', vol. 2, p. 397 (November 1837).

Prose in the *Rugby Magazine* assumed to be Clough's:
'Introductory', vol. 1, pp. 9-14 (July 1835); 'Ten Minutes before Locking Up', vol. 1, pp. 91-95 (July 1835); 'Macaulay's Battle of Ivry', vol. 1, pp. 123-132 (October 1835); 'October', vol. 1, pp. 199-205 (October 1835); 'School Society', vol. 1, pp. 207-215 (January 1836); 'A Long Talk', vol. 1, pp. 311-319 (April 1836); 'Henry Sinclair or, 'Tis Six Years Ago', vol. 2, pp. 56-61 (July 1836); 'May it please Your Royal Majesty', vol. 2, pp. 103-104 (July 1836); 'The Rugby Register', vol. 2, pp. 105-111 (December 1836); 'A Peripateticographical Article', vol. 2, pp. 223-234 (July 1837); 'Sonnets in the Abstract', vol. 2, pp. 270-274 (July 1837); 'Two Autumn Days in Athens', vol. 2, pp. 345-358 (November 1837); 'Address of Leave-Taking', vol. 2, pp. 398-400 (November 1837).

Collected Editions, Poetry and Prose (a selection):

POEMS, with a Memoir by F. T. Palgrave (1862)
—edited by the poet's wife. Second edition, enlarged, 1863; edited by C. Whibley, 1913.
LETTERS AND REMAINS (1865)
—privately printed. Contains the first complete version of 'Dipsychus'.
THE POEMS AND PROSE REMAINS, 2 vols. with a selection from his Letters and a Memoir, edited by his wife with J. A. Symonds (1869)
—reprinted 14 times before 1902. The Prose Remains were reprinted separately in 1888.
THE POETICAL WORKS: With a Memoir by F. T. Palgrave (1906)
—in the Muses' Library.
THE POEMS, edited by H. F. Lowry, A. L. P. Norrington, and F. L. Mulhauser, Oxford (1951)

—the definitive edition with Oxford English Texts from which all titles and quotations in the present essay have been taken.

Collected Prose (a selection):

PROSE REMAINS OF A. H. CLOUGH, with a selection from his letters and a memoir: edited by his wife (1888).

EMERSON–CLOUGH LETTERS, edited by H. F. Lowry and R. L. Rusk. Cleveland (1932).

CORRESPONDENCE, edited by F. L. Mulhauser, 2 vols., (1957).

Selected Works:

SELECTIONS FROM THE POEMS OF A. H. CLOUGH (1894)
—in the Golden Treasury Series.

THE BOTHIE AND OTHER POEMS, edited by E. Rhys (1896).

POEMS, including 'Ambarvalia', both versions of 'The Bothie', 'Amours de Voyage' etc., edited by H. S. Milford (1910)
—contains, in the editor's Preface, the best account of Clough's hexameters.

Separate Works:

THE LONGEST DAY: A Poem written at Rugby School (1836).

THE BOTHIE OF TOPER-NA-FUOSICH: A Long-Vacation Pastoral, Oxford (1848)
—Clough subsequently changed the title to "Tober-na-Vuolich" and a revised version of the poem appeared in *Poems* 1863.

AMBARVALIA: Poems by T. Burbidge and A. H. Clough (1849)
—Clough's contributions were re-issued as a separate volume (without a title leaf) in 1850.

AMOURS DE VOYAGE [first published serially in *The Atlantic Monthly* Boston, Mass., Feb.-May, 1858, and first printed as a whole in *Poems*, 1862.]

DICTIONARY OF GREEK AND ROMAN BIOGRAPHY AND MYTH, edited by W. Smith, 3 vols. (1844-49)
—Clough contributed seventy seven short biographies to the first two volumes. Each article is signed "A.H.C.".

ILLUSTRATIONS OF LATIN LYRICAL METRES. (Classical Museum, IV 1846). See "New Verses by Clough", by G. Tillotson (*The Times Literary Supplement*, June 18th, 1954).

POEMS AND BALLADS OF GOETHE. *Fraser's Magazine* LIX (1859). Review of "Poems and Ballads of Goethe", translated by W. E. Aytoun, D.C.L., and T. Martin (1859).

GREEK HISTORY FROM THEMISTOCLES TO ALEXANDER in a series of Lives from Plutarch. Revised and arranged (with a Preface) by A. H. Clough (1860).

PLUTARCH'S LIVES. The translation called Dryden's, corrected from the Greek and revised (with an introduction) by A. H. Clough, 5 vols. Boston (1864, 1874, 1876, 1902): edited by E. Rhys, 3 vols. Everyman's Library (1910).

Some Critical and Biographical Studies:

ON TRANSLATING HOMER, by M. Arnold (1861)
—contains some illuminating asides on *The Bothie.*

ESSAYS, THEOLOGICAL AND LITERARY II, by R. H. Hutton (1877)
—contains commentary on Clough.

LITERARY STUDIES II, by W. Bagehot (1879)
—contains a perceptive and sympathetic study of Clough.

ARTHUR HUGH CLOUGH: A MONOGRAPH, by S. Waddington (1883)
—the first full-length study.

LITERARY ESSAYS, by R. H. Hutton (1888).

PORTRAITS OF FRIENDS, by J. C. Shairp (1889)
—contains Shairp's contribution to the Memoir, prefixed to Poems and Prose Remains.

STUDIES IN INTERPRETATION, by W. H. Hudson (1896).

NEW ESSAYS TOWARDS A CRITICAL METHOD, by J. M. Robertson (1897).

FAITH AND DOUBT IN THE CENTURY'S POETS, by R. A. Armstrong (1898).

ENGLISH TALES IN VERSE, by C. H. Herford (1902).

MISCELLANEOUS ESSAYS AND ADDRESSES, by H. Sidgwick (1904).

BRIEF LITERARY CRITICISMS, by R. H. Hutton (1906).

ENGLISH LITERATURE IN ACCOUNT WITH RELIGION, by E. M. Chapman (1910).

FOUR POETS: Clough, Arnold, Rossetti, Morris, by S. A. Brooke (1913).

ESSAI SUR LA FORMATION PHISOSOPHIQUE DU POETE CLOUGH: Pragmatisme et Intellectualisme, par E. Guyot. Paris (1913).

ARTHUR HUGH CLOUGH, by J. I. Osborne (1920).

STUDIES IN VICTORIAN LITERATURE, by S. T. Williams. New York (1923).

EIGHT VICTORIAN POETS, by F. L. Lucas (1930).

POETRY AND THE CRITICISM OF LIFE, by W. H. Garrod (1931).

PORTRAITS, by D. MacCarthy (1931).

THE EIGHTEEN SIXTIES, edited by J. Drinkwater (1932)
—contains an essay on Clough by H. Wolfe. Wolfe develops a new
approach to Clough and interprets him as outstandingly a satirical
poet.

THE LONELY WAYFARING MAN, by T. Scudder (1836).

ARTHUR HUGH CLOUGH, by G. Levy (1938).

THE DARKLING PLAIN, by J. Heath-Stubbs (1950).

BOOKS IN GENERAL, by V. S. Pritchett (1953).

THE DOCTOR'S DISCIPLES, by F. J. Woodward (1954).

ARTHUR HUGH CLOUGH: The Uncommitted Mind, by K. Chorley.
Oxford (1962)
—an authoritative biography. The most sensitive and sympathetic
discussion of Clough's work yet to appear.

Critical and Biographical Essays in Periodicals (a selection):

Nineteenth Century Periodicals:

'Review of the Bothie of Toper-na-Fuosich' (i.e. Tober-na-Vuolich),
by C. Kingsley. (*Fraser's Magazine,* 1849).

'Review of the Bothie of Toper-na-Fuosich' (i.e. Tober-na-Vuolich),
by W. M. Rossetti. (*The Germ,* I, 1850).

'Clough's Poems', by D. Masson (*Macmillan's Magazine,* 1862).

'Arthur Hugh Clough', by F. T. Palgrave. (*Fraser's Magazine,* 1862).

'Arthur Hugh Clough', by J. A. Symonds. (*Fortnightly Review,* 1868)
—a particularly penetrating discussion of Clough's work.

'Arthur Hugh Clough', by J. Dowden. (*Contemporary Review,* 1869).

'Balliol Scholars: A Remembrance', by J. C. Shairp. (*Macmillan's
Magazine,* 1873)
—a poem which begins with a description of Clough very like
Matthew Arnold's 'Thyrsis' in tone.

'Arthur Hugh Clough: A Sketch', by T. Arnold. (*Nineteenth Century,*
1898).

Twentieth Century Periodicals:

'A Study of Clough's Mari Magno', by A. M. Turner. (*Publications of
the Modern Language Association,* XCIV, 1929).

'A Balliol Scholar', by M. Kent (*Criterion,* July 1830).

'Was Clough a Failure?', by F. W. Palmer. (*Philological Quarterly,*
XXII, 1943).

'The Bearing of Science on the Thought of Arthur Hugh Clough', by F. W. Palmer. (*Publications of the Modern Language Association*, LIX, 1944).

'Clough's Love and Reason', by F. L. Mulhauser. (*Modern Philology* XLII, 1954).

'A. H. Clough', by E. Underwood. (*Times Literary Supplement*, 8th September 1945).

'Victorian Verse Novels', by I. Macdonald. (*The Listener*, 16th March 1950).

'Clough as Dipsychus', by K. Badger. (*Modern Language Quarterly* XII, 1951).

'Clough at Oriel and at University Hall', by G. P. Johari. (*Publications of the Modern Language Association* LXVI, 1951).

'Clough: The Shorter Poems', by D. N. Dalglish. (*Essays in Criticism* II, 1952)

—a demonstration of the vigour and energy of Clough's shorter poems. Clough's reputation improved after the authoritative edition of his poetry appeared in 1951. There was a renewal of scholarly and critical interest in his work, and the following essays attempt to reach a closer understanding of his life and poetry.

'Clough's Amours de Voyage', by J. D. Jump. (*English* IX, 1953).

'Un Regain d'interest pour Arthur Hugh Clough', par P.Veyriras. (*Etudes Anglaises* XI, 1958).

'Arthur Hugh Clough's Formative Years: 1819-1841', by R. Gollin. (*Dissertation Abstracts XX*, 1959).

'Arthur Hugh Clough: A Portrait Retouched', by M. Timko. (*Victorian News Letter* XV, 1959).

'The 'True Creed' of Arthur Hugh Clough', by M. Timko. (*Modern Language Quarterly* XXI, 1960).

'Amours de Voyage: Substance or Smoke?', by M. Timko. (*English* XIII, 1960).

'Arthur Hugh Clough: A Hundred Years of Disparagement', by W. E. Houghton. (*English Studies* I, 1961).

Miscellaneous Works relevant to Clough and his circle:

Clough's Family:

A MEMOIR OF ANNE JEMIMA CLOUGH, by B. A. Clough (1897)

—Anne Clough was Clough's only sister. This biography contains extracts from Anne's early journal, many concerned with Arthur Hugh.

The Arnolds:

THE LIFE AND CORRESPONDENCE OF THOMAS ARNOLD, D.D., late
Headmaster of Rugby School, by A. P. Stanley, 2 vols. (1844).

TOM BROWN'S SCHOOLDAYS, by T. Hughes (1857)

—its naive view of Dr. Arnold's aims fostered the belief that Arnold
represented nothing but a complacent moral earnestness.

EMINENT VICTORIANS, by L. Strachey (1918)

—an iconoclastic attack on Dr. Arnold and his influence, contains
some satirical remarks on Clough.

Matthew Arnold:

THE LETTERS OF MATTHEW ARNOLD TO ARTHUR HUGH CLOUGH, edited
by H. F. Lowry (1932)

—invaluable for Arnold's view of Clough's poetry. Arnold's criticisms
still remain the best case against Clough.

MATTHEW ARNOLD, by L. Trilling (1939).

THE POETRY OF MATTHEW ARNOLD, edited by C. B. Tinker and H. F.
Lowry (1950).

WRITERS AND THEIR WORK

General Editor: BONAMY DOBRÉE

The first 55 issues in the Series appeared under the General Editorship of T. O. BEACHCROFT

Sixteenth Century and Earlier:

FRANCIS BACON: J. Max Patrick

CHAUCER: Nevill Coghill

ENGLISH MARITIME WRITING:
  Hakluyt to Cook: Oliver Warner

MALORY: M. C. Bradbrook

MARLOWE: Philip Henderson

SIDNEY: Kenneth Muir

SKELTON: Peter Green

SPENSER: Rosemary Freeman

WYATT: Sergio Baldi

Seventeenth Century:

SIR THOMAS BROWNE: Peter Green

BUNYAN: Henri Talon

CAVALIER POETS: Robin Skelton

DONNE: Frank Kermode

DRYDEN: Bonamy Dobrée

HERRICK: John Press

HOBBES: T. E. Jessop

BEN JONSON: J. B. Bamborough

LOCKE: Maurice Cranston

ANDREW MARVELL: John Press

MILTON: E. M. W. Tillyard

SHAKESPEARE: C. J. Sisson

SHAKESPEARE:

  CHRONICLES: Clifford Leach

  EARLY COMEDIES: Derek Traversi

  GREAT TRAGEDIES: Kenneth Muir

  LATE COMEDIES: G. K. Hunter

  PROBLEM PLAYS: Peter Ure

THREE METAPHYSICAL POETS:
                    Margaret Willy

IZAAK WALTON: Margaret Bottrall

Eighteenth Century:

BERKELEY: T. E. Jessop

BLAKE: Kathleen Raine

BOSWELL: P. A. W. Collins

BURKE: T. E. Utley

BURNS: David Daiches

COWPER: N. Nicholson

CRABBE: R. L. Brett

DEFOE: J. R. Sutherland

ENGLISH HYMNS: Arthur Pollard

FIELDING: John Butt

GIBBON: C. V. Wedgwood

GOLDSMITH: A. Norman Jeffares

GRAY: R. W. Ketton-Cremer

JOHNSON: S. C. Roberts

POPE: Ian Jack

RICHARDSON: R. F. Brissenden

SHERIDAN: W. A. Darlington

CHRISTOPHER SMART:
                    Geoffrey Grigson

SMOLLETT: Laurence Brander

STEELE, ADDISON AND THEIR
  PERIODICAL ESSAYS:
                    A. R. Humphreys

STERNE: D. W. Jefferson

SWIFT: J. Middleton Murry

HORACE WALPOLE: Hugh Honour

Nineteenth Century:

MATTHEW ARNOLD: Kenneth Allott

JANE AUSTEN: S. Townsend Warner

THE BRONTË SISTERS:
                    Phyllis Bentley

BROWNING: John Bryson

SAMUEL BUTLER: G. D. H. Cole

BYRON: Herbert Read

CARLYLE: David Gascoyne

LEWIS CARROLL: Derek Hudson

COLERIDGE: Kathleen Raine

DICKENS: K. J. Fielding

DISRAELI: Paul Bloomfield

GEORGE ELIOT: Lettice Cooper

ENGLISH TRAVELLERS IN THE NEAR
  EAST: Robin Fedden

FITZGERALD: Joanna Richardson

MRS. GASKELL: Miriam Allott

GISSING: A. C. Ward

THOMAS HARDY: R. A. Scott-James

HAZLITT: J. B. Priestley

G. M. HOPKINS: Geoffrey Grigson

T. H. HUXLEY: William Irvine

KEATS: Edmund Blunden

LAMB: Edmund Blunden

LANDOR: G. Rostrevor Hamilton
MACAULAY: G. R. Potter
JOHN STUART MILL: M. Cranston
WILLIAM MORRIS: P. Henderson
NEWMAN: J. M. Cameron
PATER: Iain Fletcher
ROSSETTI: Oswald Doughty
RUSKIN: Peter Quennell
SIR WALTER SCOTT: Ian Jack
SHELLEY: Stephen Spender
R. L. STEVENSON: G. B. Stern
SWINBURNE: H. J. C. Grierson
TENNYSON: F. L. Lucas
THACKERAY: Laurence Brander
FRANCIS THOMPSON: P. Butter
TROLLOPE: Hugh Sykes Davies
OSCAR WILDE: James Laver
WORDSWORTH: Helen Darbishire

Twentieth Century:

W. H. AUDEN: Richard Hoggart
HILAIRE BELLOC: Renée Haynes
ARNOLD BENNETT: F. Swinnerton
EDMUND BLUNDEN: Alec M. Hardie
ELIZABETH BOWEN: Jocelyn Brooke
ROY CAMPBELL: David Wright
JOYCE CARY: Walter Allen
G. K. CHESTERTON: C. Hollis
WINSTON CHURCHILL: John Connell
R. G. COLLINGWOOD:
                    E. W. F. Tomlin
L. COMPTON-BURNETT:
                    Pamela Hansford Johnson
JOSEPH CONRAD: Oliver Warner
WALTER DE LA MARE: K. Hopkins
THE DETECTIVE STORY IN
          BRITAIN: Julian Symons
NORMAN DOUGLAS: Ian Greenlees
T. S. ELIOT: M. C. Bradbrook
FORD MADOX FORD: Kenneth Young
E. M. FORSTER: Rex Warner

CHRISTOPHER FRY: Derek Stanford
JOHN GALSWORTHY: R. H. Mottram
ROBERT GRAVES: M. Seymour Smith
GRAHAM GREENE: Francis Wyndham
L. P. HARTLEY AND ANTHONY POW-
    ELL: P. Bloomfield and B. Bergonzi
A. E. HOUSMAN: Ian Scott-Kilvert
ALDOUS HUXLEY: Jocelyn Brooke
HENRY JAMES: Michael Swan
JAMES JOYCE: J. I. M. Stewart
RUDYARD KIPLING: B. Dobrée
D. H. LAWRENCE: Kenneth Young
C. DAY LEWIS: Clifford Dyment
WYNDHAM LEWIS: E. W. F. Tomlin
KATHERINE MANSFIELD: Ian Gordon
JOHN MASEFIELD: L. A. G. Strong
SOMERSET MAUGHAM: J. Brophy
EDWIN MUIR: J. C. Hall
J. MIDDLETON MURRY: Philip Mairet
GEORGE ORWELL: Tom Hopkinson
POETS OF THE 1939-45 WAR:
                    R. N. Currey
J. B. PRIESTLEY: Ivor Brown
HERBERT READ: Francis Berry
BERTRAND RUSSELL: Alan Dorward
BERNARD SHAW: A. C. Ward
EDITH SITWELL: John Lehmann
OSBERT SITWELL: Roger Fulford
C. P. SNOW: William Cooper
LYTTON STRACHEY:
                    R. A. Scott-James
DYLAN THOMAS: G. S. Fraser
G. M. TREVELYAN: J. H. Plumb
WAR POETS: 1914-18:
                    Edmund Blunden
EVELYN WAUGH: Christopher Hollis
H. G. WELLS: Montgomery Belgion
CHARLES WILLIAMS:
                    John Heath-Stubbs
VIRGINIA WOOLF: Bernard Blackstone
W. B. YEATS: G. S. Fraser

In Preparation:

MEREDITH: Phyllis Bartlett
J. M. SYNGE and LADY GREGORY:
                    Elizabeth Coxhead
PEACOCK: J. I. M. Stewart

THE POWYS BROTHERS:
                    R. C. Churchill
RONALD FIRBANK and JOHN
    BENJEMAN: Jocelyn Brooke